Also by Safire Rose

"Awakening to Joy."
    Chapter in: *The Power and Impact of Courageous Changemakers: Stories of Life, Love, and Business* (DiDomenico/Shalley, Hybrid Global Publishing, 2024).

"Prayer of the Changemaker."
    Poem in: *The Power and Impact of Courageous Changemakers: Stories of Life, Love, and Business* (DiDomenico/Shalley, Hybrid Global Publishing, 2024).

Awakening, Awakening

POEMS OF LIGHT
ON THE PATH OF LOVE

SAFIRE ROSE

Versions of the following poems were first published in Inner Visions (a publication of the Agape International Spiritual Center in Los Angeles, CA): "I Want to Know Something," "If I Had No Name," "An Angel Among You," "A Silent Word Spoken," "Sitting Under the Bodhi Tree," "Awakening," "Great Mother," "If I Had One Lovely Thing to Say," "The Face of God," "She Smiles," "Genuine Peace," "Maybe Tonight," "Love Yourself Deeply," "She Let Go" (in prose form), "Gather Yourself," "Be Still," and "I Am of the New" (1993-2010); and in Science of Mind magazine, a publication of Centers for Spiritual Living: "The Stirring," "The Luminous Lane," and "The Face of God" (August 2008).

ISBN: 979-8-89316-056-7 (Paperback)
ISBN: 979-8-89316-058-1 (Hardcover)
ISBN: 979-8-89316-057-4 (Ebook)

To the Presence of Love that animates all of life

and

*To the Light within that illuminates
the spiritual path of every soul.*

The journey of a thousand miles starts from beneath your feet.

—Lao-tzu, *Tao Te Ching*

Contents

Breath
Of Life

A Silent Word Spoken

The Silence among us—between us—within us.
Woven into the fabric of our lives.
A feather alighting. A candle burning.
The sun rising. A shadow retracting.
A calmness breathing.

Some things are better said in Silence.
Like this rose breaking forth from my heart.
Its sweetness illuminating. Its softness yielding.
Its wholeness loving with strength and conviction.

Like my hand opening, emptying, letting go—
restoring trust, faith, hope—releasing fear and longing.
Like my eyes beholding with clear vision what is—unsullied by what is not.
Like my understanding gently spoken in a clear language with no edges.

There was a rapid throng of words, indications,
expectations, promises, processes.
Like a steady rain upon us.
A veil of tears.
A rift of laughter.
A gutting of emotion.
A purging.
A making known.

I heard you in the Silent movement.
Listening closely.
Opening my heart to behold you just as you are—ever gleaming and unfolding.

You heard me in the Silent movement.
Reaching from behind.
Pulling me out.
Seeing the Truth.
Knowing me with your deepest heart—ever free and expanding.
Intuition nudging, prodding, laying bare.

We return to the Silence and drink again from its still waters.
A loss of words.
A letting-go of expectations, compromises, false acceptances, wanting, desire.

The fire of Silence burns.
Its dryness crackles.
Its emptiness exposes.
What binds is broken.
What pulls is forgiven.

Trust awakens and calls us forward into the void—before the beginning.
Flying forth.
Floating free.
Newness unencumbered.

We return to the Silence.
Bowing under.
Turning over.
Giving forth.
Like a flower opening—strong and vulnerable.
Surrendering again and again and again.

A primal scream.
A past forgotten.
A Truth remembered.

Let us begin again from the Silence—meeting the Presence of Love as one another.
Hello my friend.

Awakening

The Stirring

A stirring is within me, a quiet rumble, not a roar.
> It has no particular shape or form.
> It is not born of the past and does not live in the future.
> It is a movement of consciousness following a course of its own.

The stirring is for more life.
> It is for a greater expression.
> It is beyond my imagination, and unplanned.

Sometimes I try to squelch the stirring because it is uncomfortable,
but the stirring persists.
> It grows in the womb of the unknown.
> It has a life of its own.

I do not know where it will take me.
Yet I trust the movement of the stirring,
I feel the power of the stirring, and I am willing to be changed by the dance
of the stirring.

Is there a stirring within you, an unexplainable whirring inside of you?
Do not crush the stirring. Do not push the whirring away.
> It is the result of your deepest prayers.
> It is the substance of your desire to be more.
> It is love in its natural state, waiting to be used.

The stirring is the new never-birthed you.
> It is the rhythm of life sounding a new beat.
> It is the calling of your own heart.

Stay close to the stirring.
It will take you far.
  It will reveal your next destination,
  unearth your next creation,
  and transform you into all you truly are.

I Am Awakening

I am awakening, awakening.
I am awakening to Your love.
I let my heart break open.
I let my joy be uncontained.
I am awakening, awakening.
I am awakening to Your love.

I am awakening, awakening.
I am awakening to Your freedom.
I let the doors of happiness open.
I let my wholeness shine.
I am awakening, awakening.
I am awakening to Your freedom.

I am awakening, awakening.
I am awakening to Your peace.
I let the stillness feed me.
I let Your calmness restore.
I am awakening, awakening.
I am awakening to Your peace.

I am awakening, awakening.
I am awakening to Your word.
I surrender to Your will.
I let the way be known.
I am awakening, awakening.
I am awakening to Your word.

I am awakening, awakening.
I am awakening to Your Good.
I let the floodgates of heaven open.
I let Your plenty be revealed.
I am awakening, awakening.
I am awakening to Your Good.

I am awakening, awakening.
I am awakening to Your mercy.
I forgive myself for what has passed.
I transform my anger into self-love.
I am awakening, awakening.
I am awakening to Your mercy.

I am awakening, awakening.
I am awakening to Your beauty.
I see with clearer insight. I let my heart touch.
I am awakening, awakening.
I am awakening to Your beauty.

I am awakening, awakening.
I am awakening to Your light.
I embrace the empty spaces. I let myself expand.
I am awakening, awakening.
I am awakening to Your light.

I am awakening, awakening.
I am awakening to my greatness.
I let the light illumine. I let the shadows of doubt subside.
I am awakening, awakening.
I am awakening to my greatness.

I am awakening, awakening.

Inward Call

Gather Yourself

I gather myself to myself, holding myself close.
Letting the winds of change pass through me.

I am the "I" of the storm.
I am the "I" of my inner awareness.
I am That.

I gather myself to myself, holding myself close;
Severing the ties that bind me to the past and releasing future expectations.
I let myself be here now.

I gather myself to myself, holding myself close.
I hear the ancient ones calling me inward.
 To the sound of awakening.
 To the rhythm of remembering
 To the cadence of my soul's calling.

I turn around, I turn away, I turn within and rest.

I gather myself to myself, holding myself close.
I move into the mystery.
I expand into the Self.
I extend beyond the barriers of time and space.
I let myself soar freely.

I gather myself to myself, holding myself close.
I listen and let myself be spoken through.
I hear and let myself be heard.
I see and let myself be seen.

I let loose of all restrictions.
I step out of every box.
I release my attachment to the god of false opinion.
I release the ways that keep me hidden, keep me under, keep me down.

I dance. I sing. I rejoice. I am free.

I gather myself to myself, holding myself close.
My roots are planted deeply.
My branches opened wide.
I touch the heavens with my smile.
I let my real Self shine.

I gather myself to myself, holding myself close.
I honor my authentic flow.
I let the truth be known.
I am willing. I am able. I am available to Spirit.

My Destiny

Heavenly Father,
Divine Mother,
All That Is,
I am listening.

I hear your sweet something, I hear your sweet nothing. I hear it all.
I hear you in the stillness of morning when day breaks, the first bird sings, and my eyes open.
In that moment between night and day, I turn toward you and share my heart completely.

A prayer on my lips speaks to a presence that has carried me through the night and invites me into a new day.
A blank slate of endless possibilities.
I bless each possibility as it flows through me.
I am healed by your presence.
Like the scent of a rose, you fulfill me even though I cannot see or touch you.

I let go of everything that has come before this moment, so that I may stand in your presence and shine as your glory.
Because you shine as me, I can simply be.
I no longer have
     To do something
         To become something
            To do something else.
I am enough in the light of your love, and in service to your calling.
Infused with your presence, I enter the world as an emissary of peace, an ambassador of joy, a harbinger of hope, and a font of well-being.
My expression is a reflection of my divine connection.

It's not about me, it's about my destiny.

It's about yielding to a movement within me that is so compelling it uproots my selfish attachments and unleashes a reservoir of spiritual abundance within me.

More life. More freedom. More love.

I let the source of All That Is guide me and grow me.

As I surrender my egoic self, I subsume many little desires for the one desire:

To know you, to show you and to represent you.

I accept my spiritual destiny with every cell of my being because you have given me permission

> to be here in this moment,

> to speak this word,

> and to glorify you with my light and my love.

Oh, I surrender it all, and I surrender my surrender.

I Want to Know Something

I want to know something.
Not what I've been told to believe.
Not what I've learned from a textbook, a lecture, a story, a sermon.
I want to know something—something that rips my heart open with its truth.

I want to know something
more real to me than the chair that I am sitting on.
A truth that propels me forward.
A life that lives me from the inside out . . . peels back the layers of deception
I have been living in.
I want to know something earth-shaking, mind-blowing, heart-altering,
soul-stirring.

I want to know something.
Something so real that I can say for sure that what I say—
I know. And what I know is true.

I want to know something,
        just for me,
        just for a moment,
        just to be certain.
I want to know something that will dismantle my maybes,
transform my doubts, and dismiss the unexacting, and unexamined theories
about my life.

I want to know something; just a little . . . something.

A truth that is true for me.

A truth that isn't manufactured.

A hand-made truth.

A truth that is worth knowing.

A truth that is worth living.

A truth whose colors won't fade in the washing machine of time.

I want to know something that causes my head to turn when I hear it.

I want to know something from the bottom up.

I want to know something—and to trust the very thing I know with all my heart.

If I Had No Name

If I had no name, would you know who I am?
Or would I be a number, a title, a doer of duties?
If I had no home, would you know who I am?
Or would I be nowhere, non-existent, lost, or invisible?

If I had no past, no memory, no stories, or pictures,
would you know who I am?
Or would I be a space, a probability, or a character you once read about?

If I had a problem, a koan, an unsolvable dilemma,
would you know who I am?
Or would you ignore me, try to fix me, or silence my confusion?

If I had no plan, no direction, and no agenda, would you know who I am?
Or would you hurry my waiting,
define my wanting,
direct my desires?

If I was needy, insecure, or unsteady,
would you know who I am?
Or would I be a burden, a victim, or an object of further inquiry?

If I had no words, just an idea with no expression, would you know who I am?
Would you listen to my meaning?
Watch my hands, look into my eyes?

If I was crying and in distress, would you know who I am?
Would you sit with me in the stillness, be with me in the moment?

If I had no face, no limbs, or was lost or abandoned, would you know who I am?
Would you touch me, know me, be with me, or hold me?

If I had no body, just a smile in deep space, would you know who I am?
Would you laugh with me, cry with me, fly with me, wonder?

If I had no name, would you know who I am?

Spiritual Allies

An Angel Among You

There is an angel who walks among you.
The woman who opens the door before you.
The man knitting and sewing, giving gifts of the heart to keep you warm.
The child rolling over the grassy knoll, reminding you that you are never too old.

There is an angel who walks among you.
The wind that whispers in the quiet of day,
"I love you, you can do this, let me show you the way."
The full moon at night that winks the dark away.

There is an angel who walks among you.
The co-worker who helps you to meet your deadline on time.
The plumber who repairs your pipes in the middle of the night.
The store clerk who carries the groceries to your car.

There is an angel who walks among you.
The friend who advises you when you go astray.
The stranger who tells you help's on the way.
The healer who prays for you, night and day.

There is angel who walks among you.
The teacher who speaks the truth, beyond right and wrong.
The mentor who changes the course of your life.
The lover who sees you in God's holy light.

There is an angel who walks among you.
The named and the nameless;
The friend and the foe;
The generous and the withholding.

Each one helps you to remember the Presence of Love.
Each one reminds you, you are never alone.
Each one is an angel who walks among you.
Open your heart, and behold the hands and feet of God!

Circle of Prayer

We came, every one of us, to sit circle, and pray for our beloveds.
Placing before us the names of those who had passed to the other side:
Robert and Alice, Olive and Theodosia, Charles and Lavada.
Pillars of light, hearts of love, hands of service.

We prayed about them and for them, in waves of whispers.
Our voices circled around us as we called each soul to the center.

We prayed, every one of us, a spontaneous prayer,
each from our heart,
and our words flowed freely.

We blessed them,
we thanked them,
and we released them, onward.

Some of us prayed like the red earth, roots running deep.
Some of us prayed like the blue sky, expanding light above.
Some of us prayed like the flaming fire, burning the dross of misperception.
Some of us prayed like the clear water, rejuvenating all.

We prayed, every one of us, for ourselves as well.
    Holding tender the remembrance of what connects each to the other.

We prayed for our community, its idea unfolding
    in this year, years gone by, and in the years to follow.
We prayed, every one of us, soul sisters and brothers,
    holding one another in the embrace of our innermost thoughts.

We came, every one of us, to sit circle, and pray for our beloveds.
Placing before us the names of those who had passed to the other side:
Robert and Alice, Olive and Theodosia, Charles and Lavada.
Pillars of light, hearts of love, hands of service.

The Silent Ones

The silent ones are with you. They're not judging you.
They see beyond the patterns of this world into the possibility of now,
Creating the space for you to come into yourself, with strength and power and freedom,
Beholding you, and holding for you,
That you may discern the upward path before you.

The silent ones are knowing you.
Knowing, not controlling, you.
They are opening inner doors so you can walk through outer doors with grace and ease.

The silent ones are loving you
With an unconditional love that is not afraid to speak the truth, when necessary,
To speak the truth when you have forgotten your hopes, your dreams, your aspirations,
When you have lost track of your essential nature.

The silent ones are seeing you.
Seeing the beauty of you into creation.
Seeing the strength of you into purpose.
Seeing the expansion of you beyond space and time—or human expression.

The silent ones are comforting you
With prayers of complete peace, words of utter joy, with a truth that is resounding.
They show you windows of opportunity,
Open you to pathways of no resistance,
Help you to befriend the ones that see you clearly and love you dearly.

The silent ones are with you and speak when you call upon them.
With words of knowing, they surround you in compassion, as you navigate life.
They perceive your wholeness and true being.
They loosen your attachments so you can move more freely.
They encourage inspired action.

The silent ones illuminate the helpful course correction.
They are with you.
Guiding you and enlivening you.
Reminding you to laugh and not to struggle.
To celebrate life as it is.

I Bow to The Mother in All Things

I bow to the Mother in all things.
The night that breaks into day.
The birds that sing me awake.
The nourishing food on my plate.
I bow to the Mother in all things.

I bow to the Mother in all things.
The earth that supports my feet as I walk.
The silence that reveals its peace as I pray.
The order that structures my working day.
I bow to the Mother in all things.

I bow to the Mother in all things.
The light that illumines my darkest night.
The joy in me that bubbles up unprovoked.
The tears that cleanse and make me whole.
The celestial song that sings my soul.
The hug that reminds me I'm never alone.
The kindness bestowed in a friendly "hello."
I bow to the Mother in all things.

I bow to the Mother in all things.
I bow to the new born out of the old.
I bow to the eternity in back of each finite day.
I bow to the friends who have passed away.

I bow to the conditions that have helped me to grow.
I bow to the mystery of it all.
I bow to the infinite variety of the divine in flesh.
I bow to the preciousness of this very breath.
I bow to the Mother in all things.

Pivot Of Faith

Maybe Tonight

Maybe tonight, maybe just this one moment,
    I will turn back the hand of time and forgive myself.
    I will tear myself from the torn and yellowed pages of my past,
    wipe these fraught-filled tears of fears about the future, and love myself.
    I will contemplate how the lines and circles on my fingertips
    form a unique unrepeatable configuration.

Maybe tonight, maybe just this one moment,
    I will open to the thousands of prayers, acts of kindness,
    and beautiful blessings that have come my way, and embrace them fully.

Maybe tonight, maybe just this one moment,
    I will rise above my errant thinking and turn my awareness toward Love's
    holy beholding of me.
    I will repeal the attitudes and effects that have pockmarked my
    self-esteem with a laundry list of superficial inadequacies,
    and let the untamed waters of my soul's eternal longing
    emerge to flourish and flow as me.

Maybe tonight, maybe just this one moment,
    I will let this river of redemption carry me to my next destination without
    remediating,
    squelching,
    or destroying
    the one true thing about me.

Against the backdrop of a thousand screaming No's,
    I will renounce my resistance to loving my life fully and I will dwell in an eternal moment of gratitude so deep and soul-quenching that even the shadows of my false selves will fade in the light of my resolution of true self-beholding.

Maybe tonight, maybe just this one moment,
    I will declare my sincere love of self
    and affirm my right to be to such a degree that my authentic self-expression cannot help but shine, touching me and transforming all those around me.

Maybe tonight, maybe just this one moment, I will love myself.

Great Mother

Great Mother of all realms and dimensions,
>	wrap your arms around my broken heart and let me grieve.

Let me lay down the sword that keeps me battling myself and prevents me from expressing my underlying goodness.

Let me release this sense of separation,
>	like a crack going through my heart,
>	a great chasm between then and now,
>	between me and other,
>	between me and you.

Carry me across this chasm of separation and let the tears of grieving cleanse and release that which no longer serves me.

Great Mother, undivided one,
Reveal the inner wholeness of my being.
Let the broken pieces of days gone by,
>	of seeming failures,
>	of unreconciled moments,
>	melt in the fire of your divine grace.

Am I listening?
I let myself be distracted by so many things,
>	like this joy camouflaged as fear
>	camouflaged as anger.

I feel the broken pieces within me warring for my attention.

Let me remember that the part of me witnessing this war of fictional factions is completely whole and imperturbable.

Great Mother,
Enfold me in your wings of mercy.
Let me cry a thousand tears for those who have passed,
     for those who have suffered,
     for those who have forgotten.

Oh, Great Mother,
Restore to me the eyes of fresh seeing
     that I may look upon this world with its poverty, riches, hunger, and war,
and perceive your presence undergirding all.

Let me remember your equanimous smile stretching across the sea of samsara and consuming the night with the light of your generous glowing.

Help me to flow with the rhythm of change and ride the wave of your cyclical unfolding.
Creation. Preservation. Dissolution. Release.
A divine seamstress, you unerringly cut away what is no longer needed, revealing life's perfect pattern.

Divine Mother, source of all.
Wipe away the tears of resentment and bitterness from my eyes.
Warm my brow with your tender caress.
Let me relax into your divine embrace.
Release me from worries, cares, and concerns, the how-to's, when's, and why's.
     Let me dance in your ever-effulgent joy and abundance.
     Let me know myself as fully and completely as you know me,
          unencumbered, with conscious appreciation and love.

Great Mother of this world and of that,

Open my heart to receive your divine blessings.

Amplify my willingness to obey your word.

Awaken me to your vision of my life.

Still me in times of turbulence, that I may radiate the light of your love.

Let me be me.

Sitting Under the Bodhi Tree

I am a woman sitting under the Bodhi tree,
sitting where the Buddha sat,
    touching the earth in the presence of Mara
    touching into a thousand lifetimes of service, meaning, and purpose.

I am a woman grieving.
Watching sadness rise and fall away,
watching dreams form and disperse.
    One tear falls from my face,
        one glimmer of hope,
        one drop of compassion,
        one watery way of plenty, all overflowing from my life.

Would one more choice make a difference?
Would I choose a better choice?
Would I stand on solid ground watching the shadows fade in the light of my
awareness?

I am a woman forgiving;
letting go of all the judgments I have held against myself.
A song of sorrow reveals a joy emerging.
    I am singing a new life.
    I am releasing old ways.
    I am beginning anew.
    I am beginning again.

I am a woman flying in freedom,
letting loose the restrictions I have put upon myself.
My love expands and fills the empty places within me with light
so that I may take flight in the glow of love's embers.

I don't need another to tell me who I am.
I don't need another to free me from self-imposed limitations.
I am turning my attention within, meeting my Self face to face
and loving from that place:
> a love unconditioned by the past,
> a love unconditioned by billboards and media blips,
> a love that frees me and those around me to be who we truly are.

I am a woman sitting under the Bodhi tree,
> sitting where the Buddha sat,
> watching the breath rise and fall,
> letting the glittery lies fade away,
> finding my way.

I am a woman sitting under the Bodhi tree,
> sitting where the Buddha sat,
> sitting still,
> and moving forward.

There Will Come a Time

There will come a time
When a thought so divine will guide you.
Like a storm passing through, grey skies will turn blue,
And the road will open wide before you.

Take a step into the unknown.
Don't let yourself be tossed or thrown.
Trust yourself as you begin the journey onward.

There will come a time
When you will leave behind
The world you have created for now.
Feet pointing forward,
Head clear and upright,
No one will be able to dissuade you any longer.

Ride on the wave of your tiny successes.
Each one of them carries you further.
Let go of the fears, wash away the tears,
Let the glee deep inside inform you.

Follow a dream you have been dreaming forever.
Even now angels gather about you.
They have your back, let go of lack—and proceed on the route before you.

The doors inside you have opened.
You'll no longer be able to close them.
No physical place will confine you.

The search will be over as the truth sounds inside you.
And the home of your heart will find you.
Enjoy this breath and leave the rest.
Let the cloud of confusion roll by you.

There will come a time.
Moments will align.
No more finger-tapping or explanations.
You'll see a sign, catch a vision sublime: Step into the heaven before you.

Touching
Presence

Be Still

There is a stillness that goes beyond silence.
It exists in the beingness of each and every moment.

Deep within all activity,
Deep within the movement of all creation,
Stillness breathes and beckons us to enter into its holy embrace.

The stillness is active and dynamic. Not stagnant or stale.

It silently reveals itself in the breaking of the dawn,
In the magic of the setting sun,
In the waxing and waning of the moon.

It actively reveals itself in the rhythm of a singer's song,
The vibration of the spoken word,
The movement of a dancer's steps.

We may sense the presence of stillness more readily when we slow down,
When we consciously breathe in and out, and when we accept things as they are,
But the energy of stillness calls us inward,
Wherever we go, whomever we are with, and whatever we do.

You may enter the stillness at any time.
It is the rich soil of your own soul calling you into a greater expression.

Immerse yourself in the stillness of this moment.
Open to its wide expanse.
Feel the energy of effortless living.

It is said, "Be still and know that I am within you."
Perhaps the converse is also true--
Touch the presence within you, and it will reveal its stilling power.

When we consciously recognize the presence of Spirit in every moment
We will experience it as the dynamic stillness at the heart of all of life.

If I Had One Lovely Thing to Say

If I had one lovely thing to say it would be about God.
A round thought with no beginning or end.
It would fall from my mouth without a stutter and would cause a ripple so profound that even the wind would change its direction.

If I had one lovely thing to say it would be about God.
A love so profound it would burn off the rough edges of my being
and dissolve my defenses;
you could see right into me, and I would not be afraid.

If I had one lovely thing to say it would be about God.
About the storm in me that has dismantled my linear thinking,
upended my life, and exposed my withholding.
There would be nothing to do but surrender my reservations about real living.

If I had one lovely thing to say it would be about God;
it would be so full of gratitude that nothing could diminish its spontaneous outpouring.

If I had one lovely thing to say it would be about God.
It would uncover the false to reveal a truth I didn't know I was hiding.
It would start as a small smile, expand into soul-filled laughter,
and make me lose all control.

If I had one lovely thing to say it would be about God.
Not a dissertation about God but merely a suggestion:

If someone hands you a glass of water and you are thirsty, drink the water.
Don't waste your time talking about its many valuable properties.

If I had one lovely thing to say it would be about God.

The Face of God

Touch the face of God;
> the face outside of you,
> the face inside of you,
> the face expressing you.

The face of God is the face you see in the mirror,
and it is the face in back of the face you see in the mirror.
The face of God is the face that watches you face your face in the mirror.

The face of God is the divine and perfect pattern of all of life.
A leaf, a flower, a cloud, a rock: each reveals the face of God.
It is the seen and unseen presence behind all of life.
It is the face of your employer, the face of your spouse,
the face of your co-worker, and the face of your "enemy."

The face of God is transcendent and immanent.
It is the face you wear on your body, and it is the divine idea behind your physical expression.

Touch the face of God that is reflected back to you in everything you see, sense and feel.
Let it become a living reality.
Let yourself peel back the layers of self-judgment, worry and doubt and be the beaming blossom of beauty that you are.

Touch the face of God as you look upon yourself;
embrace yourself with love.
Touch the face of God as another;
embrace them with the warmth and light of God's love.

If all the love in the world could be given by one face, would you accept that love?
If all the love of God could be given from your face—would you let it shine?
Would you be willing to express that love?

Touch the face of God;
        the face outside of you,
        the face inside of you,
        the face expressing you.

And let yourself be touched.

She Smiles

She smiles within me, as me, all around me;
    an eternal smile that has no beginning and no end.
Her smile lifts me up and tickles my joy into jubilation.

She smiles a knowing smile of compassion and understanding
    and reminds me of my true purpose,
beyond what I do to pay the bills.

She smiles, and Her radiance reverberates within me,
    lighting up every cell in my body,
    and orchestrating the movement of every muscle, fiber, and tissue;
It's all in Her capable hands.

Her breath breathes me,
    and like a hollow bamboo flute
    my body becomes an instrument of Her divine song.

She smiles, and I laugh for no reason.
I am giddy with Her Goodness.
In that moment, it is all worthwhile—the ups and downs of three-dimensional living,
the daily grind,
the watchful eye,
the deepening of my willingness to surrender.

She smiles, and my body is quickened,
my strength is renewed,
my intention refined,
my heart opened.

She smiles a secret smile and keeps me guessing about my Good.
We joke and muse about the life I am living; such a wonder-filled life.

She smiles, and I remember to remember
that I am here to dance and sing,
glow and glide,
and to watch my life with complete adoration.

She smiles, and I feel my oneness with all of life —
      the yellow sunflower,
      the red rose,
      the blue sky, and the silvery moon.
Every moment becomes an opportunity to give thanks.

She smiles, and I am free, childlike, and new.
She smiles Her eternal smile,
and once again the smile that smiles all of life
smiles as me.

Into The Light

The Luminous Lane

There is a luminous lane within you:

   a lane of possibility,

   a lane of no limitation,

   a lane of right action.

You may step into this lane at any moment, but you must be aware, and you must act quickly.

There is no time for doubt or hesitation.

You must trust yourself completely.

Someone speaks and before you react, turn within.

From within, your desire to be more expands,

and the gap between what is said and what follows reveals a golden hue.

Like a beacon drawing you inward, this golden gap of opportunity carries you to the luminous lane,

the luminous lane of your own heart.

There are no yesterdays in the luminous lane.

There are no tomorrows.

Even the present does not exist in the luminous lane.

There is only the NOW.

As you choose the luminous lane it widens to accommodate the growing strength and power of your intention.

   You are standing in the light of infinite possibilities.

   You are standing in a place of expanded awareness.

   You are seeing yourself knowing yourself as you choose your next moment.

In the luminous lane, your real self-shines.

    You are teachable, pliable, willing, and more.

    You are clear, open, happy, and free.

Possibilities emerge because there is nothing to fear.

Limitation dissolves because there is nothing to resist.

The deepest desires of your heart reveal perfect right action.

In the luminous lane, the loving words that you want to speak are spoken.

The peaceful response that you want to make is made.

The gentle touch that you want to give is given.

Become aware of the golden gap arising before you, the space between opportunity and action.

Turn within.

Step out of your habitual reactions and into the luminous lane of creative response.

From this place, choose into more of you.

Genuine Peace

My anger has made me peaceful.
The slow movement of awareness upon awareness.
Remembering to remember
        has allowed a tenacious and tender love to emerge.

"Let me become even bigger."
"Use me," I say to myself.
In the midst of any frustration,
in the midst of any resentment,
in the midst of any hurt,
I am pulled ever inward.
Spirit calls itself to me.
It sings itself softly through me:
"Remember Me, remember Me, come onto Me."

My anger has made me peaceful.
The slow movement of awareness upon awareness.
Let the tone of my voice soothe instead of threaten.
Let my words comfort instead of distance.
Let my actions serve instead of self-serve.
This is the prayer of my heart.

My anger has made me peaceful.
The slow movement of awareness upon awareness.
Let me remember to remember and let that remembrance come quickly.
Let me release the struggle to make myself different.
Let me release the struggle to change the situations around me.

Let me release the habit pattern of controlling, manipulating, or dismissing those around me.

"I see you, Oh God. I remember you, Pure Spirit."

My anger has made me peaceful.
Within the slow movement of awareness upon awareness,
      this that I have called anger,
      this that I have known as fear,
      this that I have resisted and blamed,
      has transformed itself before my very eyes.
It is peace becoming.
It is love in disguise.
It is no longer an adversary, but an angel in my life.

Love Yourself Deeply

Love yourself deeply and completely.
Let the Spirit be your guide.
Drop all the surrogate lovers, the fantasies, and the lies, and return to yourself.
Refuse to abandon yourself any longer.

Perhaps you have searched all your life, or even lifetimes, for the one or the many who will see you clearly, understand you perfectly, and appreciate you endlessly.
It matters not.
Return to your soul center.

Let go of the search for perfect love.
Perfect your own love.
Behold the bounty of your beauty, the generosity of your joy, the sincerity of your soul.
Sparkle in the light of your own inner glory.

Hunger for the immensity of Pure Spirit, not the intensity of illusive love.
No amount of longing will awaken an unavailable lover.
Let them slumber.
Nurture yourself.

Say it once or say it a thousand times,
 "I am worthy of my own love."
 "I expand into my unlimited nature and being."
 "I am not a victim of anyone, anything, or any thought. I am free."
Say it until the floodgates of love burst open within you.
Then swim in the ocean of sunlit love.

Love yourself deeply and completely.
Let the Spirit be your guide.
Drop all your wishful thinking and trust yourself.

Step into the life God made for you.
Let go of all the hesitation and come into yourself.
Avail yourself of the One and Only Source of Love.
Be a light unto yourself.

Then ignite the world with your own effulgence.

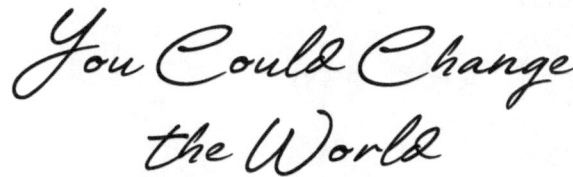

You Could Change the World

You could change the world without trying to make it better.
By following the rising and falling of your breath.
By listening to a muster of cawing crows, louder than daybreak and seemingly in distress.
If you listen without judgment or the weighing of like and dislike you could hear the crows in the dawning day, and fall in love, dissolving all separation between you.

If you stop for just one moment, put the pen down, walk away from your desk, and step outside, you might notice the simple, startling beauty before you.
Golden leaves glowing, crisp air inviting, morning glories overflowing.
Opening in and opening out, you could touch the earth with each tip of your fingers and one by one release the fears that keep you separate from the healing nourishment of the benevolent Mother.

If you stop in this now-moment, and tune into your eyes and ears, body and heart, bone and sinew, you might sense a subtle vibration:
Seagulls soaring, waves breaking on the shore, pipers tiptoeing in the sand.
Feeling that, you could dive into the ocean of love within you, surrender to its surprising undulations, and find yourself surfing the waters of your own life in a joy that is fluid and free.

If you stop for just one moment, sit still, or walk with awareness, you might feel a serene and dynamic presence within you.

You could trust that presence.

You could sink into yourself and pull out a bouquet of yesses.

A yes to living with wakeful intention.

A yes to tenderly caring to your daily needs.

A yes to reverently relating to the spontaneous expression of life—and to releasing the incessant judgments that prevent you from loving yourself and others.

A yes to detaching from the mental chatter that keeps you bound, and a yes to yielding to the inner movement of consciousness within you.

If you stop for just one moment, put your hand on your heart and notice its beat, you might feel your connection to the rhythm of life, and effortlessly step into its syncopated flow.
Rosebud opening, scent piercing, petals falling.
Touching that, you could notice your subtle resistance to the way things are and surrender your insistence on how you want things to be. In that profound release, you could ride the waves of the ephemeral in a boat made of the eternal.

If you stop for just one moment, letting the fire of discomfort burn into ease, you might witness the implicate order of all things:
Fire into rain, rain into river, river entering ocean of all.
Bringing breath and body to the tiniest sliver of time,
You could change the world.

Breaking
Free

Freedom of My Own Mind

What I want is freedom of my own mind.
To think a thing and know a thing and trust the truth of that thing to such a degree that the negative chatter of my mind does not disturb, perturb, or unnerve me.

What I want is freedom of my own mind.
To say yes to what is certain and to be so convinced of the Truth that my inner resolve dissolves all lesser thinking.

What I want is freedom of my own mind.
To sit in the chair of high thinking until I see what I know and know what I see and become unconcerned about the clanging cymbals of superficial living.

What I want is freedom of my own mind.
To consciously court the newness of what is Real and turn my attention away from the habitual thoughts of the negator, the heckler, and the incessant purveyor of mediocrity.

What I want is freedom of my own mind.
To be all that I say that I am and to unequivocally accept the harmonious thoughts that naturally emanate from within me.

What I want is freedom of my own mind.
To choose loving kindness over righteousness, authenticity over convention, and true peace over the false peace promised by the urge to control or fix a situation.

What I want is freedom of my own mind.
To take dominion over my attention and become gratefully aware of the little things that accentuate the important.

What I want is freedom of my own mind.
To realize the good and choose the good so the generosity of my own heart is unimpeded by any limited thinking.

What I want is freedom of my own mind.

Like a Wild Horse

Be like a wild horse.
Let your spirit run free.

Drop every name you have been given.
Every differentiation.
Every category imposed upon you.
Resist the temptation to trade one distinction for another.

Perhaps you go by she, he, they, or ze.
Celebrate your uniqueness but loosen your identification.
Unbridle yourself from naming conventions.

Be like a wild horse.
Unfettered and free.
The tighter you hold on, the more restricted you become.
Think about it, but not too long.

Everything can change in an instant.
Moses never entered the promised land.
Jesus was betrayed by a friend.
Joan of Arc died at the stake.
Siddhartha Gautama became awake.
Ram was exiled to the forest green.
Sita embraced her inner sovereignty.

Each life was transformed.
Each soul was undiminished.

Stay in the qualitative.

It is infinite.

Neither right nor wrong.

When you identify with the spiritual, you gain the eternal.

Be like a wild horse.

Run free and don't look back.

Be so true to yourself that you are unaffected by the name-calling of others.

Name yourself.

Name yourself good.

Name yourself good enough.

Name yourself magnificent.

Name yourself extraordinary.

Then walk in wisdom, trot in triumph, gallop in glory.

Be like a wild horse.

Say nay to the naysayers.

Transcend time and all of its notions.

She Let Go

She let go.
Without a thought or a word, she let go.
She let go of the fear.
She let go of the judgments.
She let go of the confluence of opinions swarming around her head.
She let go of the committee of indecision within her.
She let go of all the right reasons.
Wholly and completely, without hesitation or worry, she just let go.

She didn't ask anyone for their advice.
She didn't read a book on how to let go.
She didn't research the scriptures.
She just let go.

She let go of all of the memories that held her back.
She let go of all of the anxiety that kept her from moving forward.
She let go of the planning and all of the calculations about how to do it just right.

She didn't promise to let go.
She didn't journal about it.
She didn't write the projected date in her Day-Timer.
She made no public announcement and put no ad in the paper.
She didn't check the weather report or read her daily horoscope.
She just let go.

She didn't analyze whether she should let go.
She didn't call her friends to discuss the matter.
She didn't do a five-step Spiritual Mind Treatment.
She didn't call the prayer line.

She didn't utter one word.
She just let go.

No one was around when it happened.
There was no applause or congratulations.
No one thanked her or praised her.
No one noticed a thing.
Like a leaf falling from a tree, she just let go.

There was no effort.
There was no struggle.
It wasn't good and it wasn't bad.
It was what it was and it is just that.

In the space of letting go, she let it all be.
A small smile came over her face.
A light breeze blew through her.
And the sun and the moon shone forevermore.

Joyful
Abiding

I Am of the New

I am of the new, not of the old.
Old ideas, old habits, old ways of thinking
have burned in the fire of my longing to be more.

I am of the new, not of the old.
The old has been uprooted.
New seeds have been sown.
Tender sprouts spring out of the ground and grow toward the sunshine of my vision.
My heart is open wide.

I am of the new, not of the old.
I see the Illumined One everywhere.
An inner effulgence expresses as me.
I am moving in the light, breathing in the light, being in the light.

I am of the new, not of the old.
A new language forms on my lips, new words flow from my mouth:
Rose petal.
   Dewdrop.
      Sunbeam.
         Rainbow.

My words radiate in a spectrum of electric hues.
Gold, sapphire, and ruby words spill out of my mouth, all aglow and laughing.
The laughter is contagious.
Anyone who hears my words begins to smile and remembers:
"Oh love, oh joy, oh kindness, oh beauty."

I am of the new, not of the old.
My wingspan is infinite, my colors varied.
Breathing in, I am a golden hue.
Breathing out I am sapphire blue.
Every step I take is sprinkled with glitter.
Every action I make sparkles with well-being.

I am of the new, not of the old.
Old structures crumble around me.
New structures emerge out of nothing; they are light-filled and seen with the inner eye.

I am of the new, not of the old.
A new being, I am formed from within.
Loving without wanting,
acting without attachment,
knowing without thinking,
growing without effort.

I am of the new, not of the old.
A spontaneous goodness reveals itself as me.
A glorious glow radiates all about me.
I am here.
I am home.
I am free.

I am of the new, not of the old.
I walk, speak, think, and know in a new way.
The Illumined One lives within me *as* me.
My life is aglow with the Light of Love.

Come Forward

Come forward.
Into the breath of life.
Into the breath of love.
Into the breath of peace.
Ground yourself,
Feet touching earth, hands touching sky.

Come forward.
Into the joy of your heart.
Given, not earned.
Abundant and overflowing
Undisturbed.
Unaffected by the chaos of the world.

Come forward.
Into the integrity of your own heart.
No longer peddling yourself to every distracting phenomena.
Sit with yourself.
Befriend your inner demons.
Start in the middle until you reach the end.
Begin again.

Come forward.
Into the now.
Into everything that is at stake.
Make it matter.
Make it matter.
Make it matter.
Do not be concerned about the outcome or who you will be when it's over.

Pay attention to who you are now.
Cultivate trust and consistency.
Show up.
Be available.
Discern beneficent opportunity.

Come forward.
Into the Presence.
Within and all around you.
Close the heavy door behind you.
Open the skylight.
Emerge.

Joy Always Abides

Even in those moments you cannot feel it, you can know it, and in that knowing, rest.
And in that resting, you might notice.
Its imperturbable presence.

Like lying on the beach.
Pressing your whole body into the sand, back and legs, head and hair.

Like seeing with your heart-eyes the fire-lit moon illuminate the edge of each ocean wave.
Like watching each wave as it moves toward the shore.
As it moves toward you.
As it moves in you.
Breathing the moment without time or space or identity to bind you.

Awake, you see you were never asleep.

Alive, you know you were never dead.

Feeling and knowing in your bones that tomorrow you will be greeted by the morning sun.

You feel it.
Then you know it.
Then you feel it
Again.

Notes

Page 7:

Tao Te Ching, Stephen Mitchell, trans. New York: Harper & Row, 1988.

Page 32:

Generally, for me the word God represents an isness or a presence, more than a person. I use a variety of words to describe the divine (*i.e.* Spirit, All That Is, The Illumined One, Goddess, etc.) but I have discovered that any description is "a finger pointing at the moon," and falls short of capturing my full experience. That being said, in addition to experiencing the divine as beyond gender, I also experience it as inclusive of all genders.

Page 47:

As the Buddha sat under the Bodhi tree, Mara tempted him to end his focus by taunting him with the words, "Who do you think you are?" The Buddha touched the earth with his right hand and replied, "With the earth as my witness, I deserve to be here," and the earth shook and frightened Mara away.

Page 57:

The line "If all the love of God could be given from your face—would you let it shine?" is inspired by St. Francis of Assisi's *In His Sanity*. ("If all the forgiveness the heavens have known could be offered from one face, would you accept that divine pardon?").

Acknowledgments

Thank you to Christy Modita, Unity I.I., M.W., Janet Eichorst, and Anne Deidre for taking the time to review an earlier draft of this manuscript and giving me honest feedback. Thank you to poet and editor, Kary Wayson, for editing my manuscript with a keen eye and a kind heart.

Thank you to author Natalie Goldberg for her "writing practice" which I began utilizing shortly after the publication of *Writing Down the Bones*. I am also grateful for the opportunities I've had to study with Natalie, including a writing conference in Los Angeles in 1992 with Natalie, Allen Ginsberg and Annie Dillard, a haiku writing retreat with Santa Fe Workshops in 2023, and a writing retreat at Mabel Dodge Luhan House in 2024.

Unlimited gratitude to my family and friends for their loving support: Barbara H., John S. K., Fred H., Unity I.I., James C., John C. K., Dana C., Christine K., M.W., Carl W., Ryan C., Kylie K., Jake K., Ashley S., Nate R., Irma S., Peggy O., Teri R., Cathy Q., John Q., Ryan Q., Maria D., Tyler Q., Diana S., Marguerite K., Bernice H., Sarah D.; and Janet G. Knox, Daytra Hansel, Diane K., Eugene Lovick, Faye Haines, Janet Eichorst, Lorene Belisama, Michele Tashima, Sandra Williams, Terri Shields, J. A. Franco, Carol P., Renée R., Santipriya A., Marguerite L.

Deep appreciation to the following individuals and communities for their inspiration and encouragement along the way: Janet G. Knox, H.Y. Lee, Thich Nhat Hahn, Michael Bernard Beckwith and Agape International Spiritual

Center in Los Angeles, Joan Steadman, Nirvana R. Gayle, Carol Traylor, Centers for Spiritual Living, Ram Dass, Trudy Goodman, Jack Kornfield, Christiane Wolf, Mirabai Starr, Susann S., Mary Hulnick, Ron Hulnick, Alan Cohen, Marilyn Alauria and her Next Level Living community; Alexandra D'Italia, J.A., Michael D., N.L., D.L., M.A., J.M., J.R.H., and N.K.B. Thank you to Self-Publishing School for all of your support.

To Christy Modita, my love and life's partner. Who knew we would be together for tens and tens of years? Thank you for a lifetime of loving, deep friendship, and creativity. Much appreciation also for editing many first drafts of my writing over the years.

To the memory of my mother Barbara (1933-1922) who loved each of her children and grandchildren deeply, who savored all things beautiful (especially rainbows, sunsets, and full moons) and who encouraged me to "keep writing," even in the final days of her life. To the memory of my brother Jim (1959-2021), who left us much too soon, but who continues to make me smile. To the memory of my mentor and friend, Dr. Janet G. Knox.

Last, but not least, thank you to the thousands of individuals who have read and circulated my poem, "She Let Go," around the world. You inspire me by your uplifting feedback and remind me that something larger than myself is running the show.

About The Author

Safire Rose is a poet, author, teacher, and interspiritual minister.

Back in 1984 when she was 27 years old, Safire underwent a profound shift in consciousness, over the course of ten days, when she awakened to an inexplicable presence of joy that lifted her out of a life-threatening depression. The presence of that joy abides in her to this day and forms the basis of her spiritual orientation to life and her writing.

Safire has been a contributor to Agape International Spiritual Center's monthly publication, *Inner Visions*, and to Centers for Spiritual Living's *Science of Mind* magazine. Safire is best known for her poem, "She Let Go."

Safire holds degrees from the University of California, Irvine (M.A.), and from Southwestern Law School in Los Angeles (J.D.). She is an ordained minister of Agape International Spiritual Center, and Centers for Spiritual Living. Safire is a graduate of the University of Santa Monica's two-year Soul-Centered Living Certificate Program in Spiritual Psychology, Alan Cohen's Foundation for Holistic Coaching, Anne Deidre's intuitive coaching program, and a founding member of Marilyn Alauria's Next Level Living program.

Safire has been a workshop facilitator, spiritual counselor, and paralegal for over thirty years. She has also been a guest speaker at Agape International Spiritual Center in Los Angeles, several Centers for Spiritual Living, and other venues.

Safire practices presence through mindful awareness, Metta, kirtan, and communing with nature.

Safire lives with her partner, Christy, in Ventura, California. She enjoys writing, listening to jazz, photographing nature, and spending time with her many nieces and nephews.

Thank You!

As a thank you for purchasing my book, I am offering my free gift, *Five Spiritual Tools for Awakening to Joy*. I have discovered that these practice tools help me to touch the joy within me, strengthen my resilience, and allow me to navigate the ups and downs of everyday living more easily. I hope these tools support you on your journey.

If you would like your free gift, I invite you to visit safire-rose.com.

Blessings,

Safire

Before You Go...

I hope you enjoyed reading this book as much as I enjoyed putting it together. I imagine it to be a book that you can return to again and again to inspire and uplift you along the way.

I appreciate all of your feedback, and I love hearing what you have to say. Your input helps me to make the next version of this book and my future books better. I invite you to leave me an honest review on Amazon letting me know what you thought of the book.

Thank you for your presence in my life,

Safire Rose